My Little Golden Book About
Seattle

By Jennifer Liberts
Illustrated by Sonya Abby

 A GOLDEN BOOK • NEW YORK

Text copyright © 2022 by Penguin Random House LLC
Cover and interior illustrations copyright © 2022 by Sonya Abby Soekarno
All rights reserved. Published in the United States by Golden Books, an imprint of
Random House Children's Books, a division of Penguin Random House LLC, 1745 Broadway,
New York, NY 10019. Golden Books, A Golden Book, A Little Golden Book, the G colophon,
and the distinctive gold spine are registered trademarks of Penguin Random House LLC.
rhcbooks.com
Educators and librarians, for a variety of teaching tools, visit us at RHTeachersLibrarians.com
Library of Congress Control Number: 2021947493
ISBN 978-0-593-37923-3 (trade) — ISBN 978-0-593-37924-0 (ebook)
Printed in the United States of America
10 9 8 7 6 5 4 3

Hi! My name is Sammy the Salmon, and I live in **Seattle**, the largest city in the state of Washington. Seattle is known as the Emerald City because it has lots of evergreen trees that keep it green all year long.

I think of Seattle as the Rainy City because it drizzles quite a bit here! Ready for an adventure? Let's go!

Our first stop is the **Pike Place Market**. This busy market has delicious treats, such as hom bow, a soft, toasted pastry with pork or beef curry inside. Pike Place is also a great spot to find fresh food from local farmers.

My favorite area, of course, is the fish market! People come from far and wide to watch the fishmongers throw fish. My fishy friends and I have made Pike Place Market world famous!

Put on your rain boots and grab a bucket, because now we're going to explore one of Seattle's many tide pools at **Golden Gardens Park**.

At low tide, we can walk on the beach and peek under rocks to catch a glimpse of sea urchins, crabs, sea worms, and sand dollars. We might even see a red octopus hiding in a shallow!

On sunny days, I like to go to **Alki Beach** to build sandcastles, splash in the water, or fly a kite. The two-mile path along the shore is perfect for riding bikes or roller-skating. Alki Beach is known as the birthplace of Seattle because the settlers who helped build the city landed at Alki Point in 1851.

Just steps away is the **Alki Point Lighthouse.** The lighthouse was built in 1913 to help sailors travel safely around the southern point of Seattle's Elliott Bay. You can take a tour of the lighthouse—and maybe even meet a Coast Guard admiral!

Our next stop is the **Seattle Aquarium,** where we can watch a diver plunge into a 120,000-gallon tank and feed the fish. (*Yum! I hope herring is on the menu.*) The aquarium is a great place to learn how to keep our oceans healthy. There's even a special exhibit that's all about protecting salmon!

The aquarium is filled with lots of my favorite friends. Who should we visit first?

The tufted puffins . . .

some silly sea otters . . .

or a giant Pacific octopus? (*Psst!* Do you know how to make an octopus laugh? Give it *ten tickles*!)

A couple of piers away is a 175-foot-tall Ferris wheel called the **Seattle Great Wheel**.

From way up top we can see Mount Rainier, the highest mountain in Washington. Mount Rainer is a volcano! It last erupted about 1,000 years ago.

Let's take another ride, this time on the **Seattle Center Monorail**. The monorail was built for the 1962 Seattle World's Fair. It carries over two million passengers between downtown Seattle and Seattle Center every year.

Here's our stop: the **Museum of Pop Culture**, also known as MoPOP. MoPOP is filled with music, movies, and art. Come inside and play the drums in the Jam Studio and see what it's like to be a musician. Just outside, you can ride a merry-go-round, climb rope ladders, or go down a super-long slide at **Artists at Play** playground.

Let's head over to **Seattle Center**, where we can visit the **Space Needle** for a great view of the city. The super-speedy elevator will take us up, up, up, till we're 520 feet above Seattle! Once we're at the top, we can stand on **the Loupe**—the world's first revolving glass floor.

Another amazing place to visit in Seattle Center is the **Chihuly Garden and Glass Museum**. This unique spot is home to loads of colorful and imaginative glass creations made by Seattle artist Dale Chihuly.

Seattle Center is also home to the **Seattle Children's Theatre**, where we can see a play or a musical that's just for kids. After the show ends, it's time to walk to the **Seattle Children's Museum**. There are so many fun things to do—we can sculpt with clay, paint a picture, or hear a folktale about a Pacific Northwest tribe!

That was *fin*-tastic! Now I want to take you to **Seattle's Museum of Flight,** where we can see real spacecraft and airplanes. Let's imagine we are on a flight in one of the first fighter planes, or soaring through the sky in a supersonic jet. We can even explore a flight capsule designed to orbit Mars!

Our next stop is the **Woodland Park Zoo**. It has more than 900 animals from 250 different species. We can see tigers, rhinos, and penguins, and we can even feed feathered friends from Australia!

At the end of an action-packed day in Seattle, there's nothing better than a delicious picnic at **Green Lake Park**. Thank you for letting me show you around Seattle, one of the most beautiful cities in the great Northwest. I loved spending the day with you!